Muses Of Vedaa

A Mélange of Poetic Expressions

Mohua Sengupta

BookLeaf Publishing

India | USA | UK

Made with ❤ on the BookLeaf Publishing Platform
www.bookleafpub.in
www.bookleafpub.com

"To my angels in heaven, Ma and Pa, with all my love and gratitude."

Acknowledgement

This collection would not have been possible without the unwavering support of my family and friends. To my healer and shaman, Jim Rajan, thank you for your guidance and inspiration.

Preface

This collection of poems reflects the journey of my life—its joys, challenges, and the insights gained along the way. Each verse is a window into my soul, capturing moments of growth and self-discovery.

I hope these words resonate with you, offering solace, inspiration, or simply a sense of connection. Thank you for allowing me to share this journey with you. A mention here, my Di always believing in my talent and lovingly preserving all my writings.

Your encouragement means the world to me.

With gratitude,
Mohua / Vedaa

The Dreamer's Perch

She perched atop her pillow throne,
In quiet worlds all her own,
An awkward kid with tangled hair,
Softly staring, lost somewhere.

Outside the window, life would go,
Fast and loud, a buzzing show,
But she was far in lands unseen,
Where skies were purple, trees were green.

A tiny world in each small blink,
In every quiet pause to think—
Of castles tall and skies so wide,
With heroes, dragons side by side.

Her laughter felt too shy, too soft,
Her words got lost and trailed off,
But in her mind, her voice was clear,
Bold with tales no one could hear.

She knew one day her worlds would grow,
Beyond the glass, outside the window,
But for now, she'd simply sit,
And in her quiet kingdom, fit.

Beautiful World

Oh, that beautiful world of the little girl,
 Where clouds held dreams that faded with
time.
 Through years and decades of "growing up,"
 She learned to put life neatly "on track."

Unsure, she metamorphosed—
 Like water, she flowed, taking the shape

 Of everything that came her way.
 "I'm fine," "As you say," her whispered refrain.

She does not complain, she does not resist;
 With silent grace, she merely agrees.

 "Ms. Nice Girl"—that's who she became,
 The one who listens, the one who stays tame.
 The little girl who dreamed so big
 Left her Neverland far behind.

 Now a spectator of her own life,
 She watches, no longer in charge.

Oh, beautiful little girl, where did you go?
 What happened to the dreams you once
wove?

Symphony Within

In my being, conflicts reside,
Inflicting pain with intense tide.

Is this what it means to be alive?
Yes, to be alive is to strive—

Between conflict and harmony, a ceaseless
dance,
A symphony of chance.

Some notes are soft, others bold,
Harmony a fragment, not the whole.

The part cannot equate the sum;
In conflict, my truest self hums—
Raw, wounded, waiting to be seen,
Yearning for the center stage between.

Not forever, but for a while,
To heal, to rest, to reconcile.

The Whisper of Stillness

Amid the noise, the clamor, the chase,
A still voice called, a quiet space.

Not in the answers, but in the pause,
A pull toward truth, without a cause.

Through books, through words, through
silken streams,
A glimpse of life beyond mere dreams.

"Be here, be now," the whispers said,
Alive in the moment, no path ahead.

No dogma bound, no creed confined,
Just freedom's touch within the mind.

A letting go, a shedding skin,
To find the vastness deep within.
He spoke of laughter, love, and play,
Of silent nights and vibrant days.

Not a guru to follow blind,
  But a mirror to the seeking mind.
In finding Osho, I found the key—
  To open the door, to simply be.

The search dissolved, the self-grew wide,
And life became the only guide.

In My Element

I matter, I exist, I find my place.
 No longer will I shrink, no longer will I fade,
 I am who I am—here, now, unafraid.

Not spinning on life's merry-go-round,
 But steering my carriage, my purpose
profound.

 I take the call, I take the shots,
 I choose my path, weaving dreams into knots.

For I cannot pour from an empty cup,
 This mask I wear lifts me up.
 Like in an airplane, I secure my air,
 To give my best, I must first repair.

Pain to Presence

Pain struck like thunder, raw and unkind,
Shattering walls I had yet to define.

A storm within, no refuge, no guide,
Stumbling blind through life's rugged tide.

Mindfulness whispered, soft as the breeze,
"Be still, breathe deep, let go and release.
"

Moments stretched, the chaos waned,
A fleeting peace, though scars remained.

Yet I faltered, a wanderer in the haze,
Lost in loops, in life's endless maze.

Questions burned, answers eluded,
Was I seeking truth, or merely deluded?

Essence uncovered, unbound and whole,
Not a mind, not a body—just the soul.
From pain to peace, from seeking to being,
I found the beauty of simply seeing.

The journey flows, no end in sight,
But now I walk in my own light.

A dance of life, a rhythm divine,
In this moment, all is mine.

HomeComing

"I wanna go home," the heart softly cries,
 Though I'm here, surrounded by love, under familiar skies.

 Brick walls embrace me, loved ones fill the space,
 Yet my soul is restless, seeking its place.

"What do you want?" the silence implores,
 The heart whispers, unlocking hidden doors:
 "I wanna go home—to my true nature, my being,
 To the stillness within, beyond all seeing."

"I long to be, and simply just be,
 Unbound, untethered, alive, and free."
 "I wanna go home," the heart repeats,
 A quiet longing no comfort defeats.

The Moment

Amid the chaos, as life gets in the way,
 I lose the path, I can't find the ray.

 The mind chatters on, a ceaseless tide,
 The body moves—alive, or just a propified
guide?
I am not a means to an end;

 I am the start, the journey, the end.
 And then, it happens—
My attention lands on a soft spray of light,
 Dancing gently on leaves, serene and bright.

 In that stillness, I know—I am here, I am
now,
 The dream I weave unfolds somehow.

All I have is this moment, fleeting yet
profound,
 Life, moment by moment, spins round and
round

Burn

A slow burn of desires, a longing—
 Is this the arrival?
 Comfort in presence, ease in absence,
 The language of the heart, of words, of
silence.
 Is this the arrival?

Just seeing—peering into another soul,
 Connecting beyond what words can hold.
 The unspoken language of body and mind,
 Transcending, intertwining, undefined.

Slow, slow burn—
 I burn, I dance, I transform.
 In this fire, I see you.
 Slow burn, slow burn.

The woman who walks alone

Cherishing aloneness, she walks alone,
In nature's embrace, her essence is sown.
Connecting with earth, with sky, with stream,
Awake to her passions, her quiet dreams.

She befriends her demons, she knows their
names,
No shadows scare her, no inner flames.

She whispers to trees, to leaves, to wind,
Stories they share, secrets they've pinned.
Solitude cradles her, not as despair,
But a realm of freedom, light as air.

Walking alone is not to lack—
It's a chosen path, no turning back.
Her journey flows, her being's tide,
Harmony dances where truths reside.

In every step, her essence shown,
She is strength, the woman who walks alone.

The unseen path

The flutter in the stomach, the light in the
eyes,
 A path less travelled, yet somehow
recognized.
 The well-worn trail, the knot that tightens
inside—
 Is it knowing or simply knowledge implied?
Is it experience, shaped by what's been,
 Or intuition, a truth felt within?

The answer eludes, as paths intertwine,
Each step revealing a mystery, divine.

The Privilege of Discovery

She was young, she was naïve,
 Her twinkling eyes so bright, alive.
 She asked me, "Do you think there's true
love?"

 In the chaos of instant gratification, of
endless notifications—
 Is there true love?
I wanted to say,
 "True love is your essence,
 It's who you are,
 A quiet flame within you, always near.

The day you realize this,
You'll stop searching outside."

But I held back,
  Not wanting to steal from her
  The privilege of discovery—
  The privilege of pain,
  Of loving and losing,
  And of knowing.
So I smiled instead and said,
  "Yes, there is.

  And I know you'll find it."

Habit of Being Yourself

Listen to your heartbeat, steady and true,
 To the quirks and dreams that make you,
you.

 Hear your desires, your fears, your flaws,
 The quiet victories, the stumbles, the pause.

There's wisdom in this deep, silent art,
 A gentle unfolding of your truest heart.

 Get used to this voice, let it guide and
dwell—
 The habit of being yourself, wholly and well.

Musk Deer

The depth of her voice, like a vast ocean's
song,
  Enchanted me, pulled me quietly along.
  I sighed to myself, "I wish I had that voice,
  That calm, collected energy—so poised."

Her presence, serene, put my soul at ease.
  I thought, "This must be the kind of peace
  That soothes others, a balm for the weary.

  After all, aren't we all just walking each other
home?"
Her flowing, crowning glory of hair,
  Sparked a longing for beauty rare.

  Her free-spirited, individual ways,
  Lifted my heart and gave me wings to blaze.

But then one day, by the restless sea,
  I noticed the depth of my own voice in me.

  I recalled how my words could ease, console,
  How my energy, too, could quiet a soul.

The winds kissed my face as I sat alone,
Reminding me of my spirit, my own.

The pin stuck in my hair drew my mind
To its strength and thickness, uniquely mine.
Oh, Musk Deer! I whispered with a knowing grin,
"The fragrance that drives you wild is within."

Rhythm of Change

The flower that blooms must wither one day,
 Cold, lonely winters give way to sunlit displays.
 Moment by moment, life shifts and flows,
 A dance of endings and what tomorrow bestows.

On days you feel down, remember this truth:
 It's a privilege to live through life's changing hues.
 You'll ride waves of passion, of growth, of change—
 Perhaps it's just hibernation, a season to rearrange.

In moments of hopelessness, hold on and believe—
 One day, you'll look back, amazed to perceive:
 "Thank you, self, for not letting go.

Through the storm, I've blossomed—I've
grown."
For love is not constant, and neither is life,
 Ever-changing, ever-flowing, through joy and
strife.

 Embrace the tides, the shifting unknown,
 In the rhythm of change, your essence is
shown.

The Light in Your Listening

you listen—you listen to presence itself,
  To what is here, to what is now.

  You listen intently to the heartbeats, the
unrest,
  To the unspoken words, the clench of a jaw.

You hear the weight of hunched shoulders,
  The quiet avoidance in fleeting eyes.
  You notice the rubbing of palms,
  A gesture of fear, a search for safety.

And in your listening, there is comfort—
  A love as pure as the moment it holds.
  I know it will change, as all moments do,
  It will transform, as seasons renew.

But in your listening, I saw my light—
  A reflection of me, burning bright.

The Dance of Awakening

Eyes closed, the world dissolves,
A storm within begins to evolve.

Breath quickens, chaos takes form,
A tide of emotions, raw and warm.

Movement erupts, wild and free,
Unleashing what's buried, unseen by me.

The body shakes, a torrent, untamed,
The ego quivers, no need for shame.

Screams pierce the silence, laughter breaks
through,
Tears flow like rivers, cleansing and true.

Each layer stripped, each mask laid bare,
A dance with the self, tender and rare.

Then stillness descends, a quiet so deep,
The soul awakens from restless sleep.
In the void, a presence, vast and wide,
A boundless joy, no need to hide.

A journey within,
Where chaos ends and clarity begins.
A dance of surrender, a union divine,
In the depths of movement, the self aligns.

The Paradox of Eleven Minutes

In a small town, under modest skies,
A girl named Maria dreamed with her eyes.
Not of riches or fame, but something untold,
A life beyond borders, free and bold.
Ventured into a world unknown,
Chasing adventure, carving her own.

In a city of glamour, of shadows and light,
She walked a path both wrong and right.

Love became a question, a yearning ache,
A line between body and soul to break.
Eleven minutes—the fleeting embrace,
Yet a lifetime unfolds in that sacred space.

Through passion's fire and the heart's despair,
Maria sought what was hidden there.

Not in lust, nor in pain's disguise,
But in the truth that love implies.
"I see your light," he softly said,
While Maria searched, her spirit led.

Through her journey, a mirror appeared,
Revealing truths both distant and near.

Desire's depths and the soul's plea,
Entwined in her quest for what could be.
To lose, to find, to rise anew,
Her body sacred, her spirit true.

Stillness of Chaung Tzu

They rang the bell in the stillness of Chaung
Tzu Hall,
  A sound that cut through silence,
  Rising with the intensity of soothing music,
  Piercing my ears and my soul.

I closed my eyes.
  My body began to sway, side to side—
  Not my doing, but my undoing,
  A surrender to the moment,
  A falling away of control.
I collapsed onto the ground,
  Eyes still closed,
  And yet, I watched myself lying there.

  A strange, weightless presence,
  Rolling slightly,
  I kissed the earth.
The golden light arrived, filling me from
within.
  Where are you from? I wanted to ask—
  You seeped into my breath,

Flooded my pores with your radiant warmth.
I swayed again,
  Not here, yet fully present.

The observer met the observed,
  And I saw myself, as I was.
When I opened my eyes, Chaung Tzu was
motionless.

The stillness held everything.
Silent, eternal.
Tears of ecstasy flowed freely—
A journey within,
A homecoming.

Sunset by the beach

The sun set, and with it, the sky transformed,
 Hues of orange, pink, and blue spreading like
whispers.
 Was it magic, unfolding moment by
moment?
 I sat there, laughing, giggling,
 A global citizen in the truest sense.
My Spanish friend spoke of her adventures,
 Her voice carrying stories of distant lands.
 My Chinese friend shared the secrets of her
cuisine,
 Each word a doorway into her world.

And there I was, in the middle of it all,
 Feeling the weight of a dream fulfilled.
 A dream of belonging everywhere,

 Of being a person of the world.
Sharing bread,
 Exchanging glances with a stranger,
 And finding a spark of connection
 In the simplicity of being here, now.

The Sanctuary Within

My scars, my flaws, my gentleness, my claws—
All of me is here, whole and unhidden.
The rainy day holds me close,
Within the walls of my house,
And the sanctuary within myself.
I feel, I reflect, and then I settle.
The child in me watches the rain,
Wide-eyed with wonder.

The healer in me places a hand on her back,
Reassuring, grounding.

"You are safe," whispers the voice within,
"In this moment and in every moment."
As time flows, my calmness deepens.

I am the tongue—resting in the mouth,
Cradled between the teeth.

Close, yet unintrusive.
Detached, yet intimately present.
Together, but separate.

www.ingramcontent.com/pod-product-compliance
Lightning Source LLC
LaVergne TN
LVHW010938200726

843509LV00013B/2245